Romantic Budget Wedding Ideas
Where to Find Cheap Wedding Dresses, Reception Venues and More

By:

Deborah Dian

Dedication

Dedicated to my daughters and step-daughters who were each able to plan the unique and charming wedding that they desired. This book is also dedicated to my husband, who has always been the perfect Father of the Bride.

Disclaimer

Wedding dress companies, online businesses, and other retailers will go out of business from time to time. Prices of products will eventually change. The information given in this book was true at the time of publication. The basic wedding budget and planning tips will remain valid, regardless of whether or not a particular business is still in operation. However, this author bears no responsibility for businesses which may no longer exist, or product prices that may no longer be available. It is highly recommended that you comparison shop both online and in stores before making any purchases.

Table of Contents

Introduction

Very few events will be more exciting during your lifetime than your wedding day. Most brides have dreamed about this day since they were children. They have thought about the dress they would like to wear, the location of the wedding, the flowers, the cake, the music, the food and just about everything else, except the cost. Because of this, the reality of having to face limitations on their dream wedding may seem disappointing, at first. However, many brides have discovered that it is possible to have a very elegant, sophisticated, lovely wedding and still stick to a reasonable budget.

This book will take you step-by-step through the decision making process. It will start with helping you plan a workable budget. For planning purposes, we will use a very modest $6,500 budget in this book. However, you can increase or decrease the amounts as much as you want, as long as you keep the costs fairly proportional and you are certain that you have covered all the important expenses. You may also find that there are areas where you don't mind spending less, such as on wedding favors, as well as some areas where you would like to indulge yourself a little more.

This budget does not cover the cost of the honeymoon, which can vary widely from couple to couple. The purpose of this book is to help you set up a reasonable budget for the ceremony and reception that will allow you to do everything you want within the amount of money you have available to spend. In later chapters, you will find valuable information on where to shop and ways to keep your expenses down, while managing to have a wonderful celebration with your family and friends.

After the budget chapter, for example, you will find a chapter designed to assist you in finding an affordable wedding dress. This is often a major expense for the bride, and some brides will immediately go over their budget by being extravagant in this one area, alone. However, there is no reason to overspend. I assure you that many gorgeous dresses can be found at very reasonable prices, if you know where to look.

You will also find suggestions throughout this book on how to save money on bridesmaid dresses, the clothing worn by the groom and groomsmen, gifts for attendants, the reception venue, alcoholic beverages, reception music, invitations, photos and other wedding expenses. By the time you have finished reading this book, you will be ready to have a dream wedding without putting either yourself or your parents deeply into debt.

No matter who is paying for your wedding – you or your parents – knowing how to keep the budget reasonable will start your marriage off on the right foot.

$6,500 Wedding Budget

For the purpose of this book, we are going to use a $6,500 wedding budget. This is a modest amount to spend on a wedding and far below the average price of over $20,000 that is currently spent on weddings in the United States. It is possible that this is more than you can reasonably spend. If so, there are definitely ways you can cut the costs. For example, if you invite a smaller group of people to your wedding, the savings will be substantial. On the other hand, you may be able to spend a bit more. If so, simply increase the budgeted amounts proportionally.

As you look over the $6,500 budget that is broken down below, think about your personal priorities. This budget has been set up to allow you to have a formal wedding dress, as well as a reception with food, alcoholic beverages, music and dancing for about 70 people. As you look over the budget, you need to decide if these are the things that are most important to you. For example, do you want to have 70 people at your wedding, or would you be just as happy with 40 or 50? On the other hand, do you or your fiancé come from a large extended family, and feel you must invite everyone, which would mean you need to allow for more than 70 people? You can easily make adjustments to this budget, depending on your individual needs. After you have reviewed this budget, you can make the changes that you feel will best meet your goal of having the best wedding possible, while staying within your budget.

After we have gone through the basic budget, you will find a series of chapters designed to help you stay within this budget. There are chapters on finding an affordable wedding dress, reasonably priced wedding bands, discounts on attendant gifts, and affordable wedding and reception venues. As you go through the book, you will discover that it really is possible to have a beautiful and affordable wedding.

Before going any further, we need to see how your budget would work. This budget is based on spending $6,500 for the wedding and ceremony, including having 70 wedding guests, 2 female attendants, and 2 male attendants.

Attire & Beauty

The Wedding Gown & Alterations: $500.00

The Headpiece & Veil: $100.00

Bride's Shoes & Accessories: $150.00

Hair, Makeup, Manicure: $165.00

Groom's Tux Rental: $150.00

Ceremony

Church fee or Ceremony Location: $200.00

Minister's Fee: $200.00

Reception

Reception Venue & Rentals: $500.00

Food & Catering ($20.00 a person):
$1,400.00

Champagne, Wine, Beer & Soft drinks:
$500.00

Wedding Cake: $130.00

Flowers & Décor

Bride's Bouquet: $60.00

Bridesmaid Bouquets (2): $50.00

Boutonnieres: $30.00

Decorations & Centerpieces: $250.00

Wedding Favors: $130

Music

Ceremony Music: $150.00

Reception DJ: $300.00

Photos and Video

Photographer & Photos: $350.00

Videographer: $250.00

Stationery

Invitations & Reply Cards: $200.00

Thank You notes: $60.00

Wedding Rings

His Wedding Band: $200.00

Her Wedding Band: $300.00

Miscellaneous

Attendant Gifts: $100.00

Guest Bags: $75.00

Now that you have an estimated budget in front of you, it is almost certain that you will want to make some adjustments. As you go through each chapter in this book, we will explore many of the ways in which you can save money on each of these budgeted items. This budget was meant to fit the needs of the average bride and groom. It is unlikely to be the perfect fit for everyone. There may be other items you wish to change or add to the budget.

As you look over the budget, decide if there is a secret wish you have. Is there something you would really like to splurge on? There is no problem with that. You may realize that there is also an expense that you could happily reduce or eliminate. Depending on how many guests are attending, for example, you may not need to spend $1400 for food and $500 for alcoholic and non-alcoholic beverages. On the other hand, you may want to spend more on those party essentials, and reduce the amount you spend for flowers, your dress, the music or your venues. As we discuss options for saving money later in the book, you may begin to get excited about exploring all the ways you can have your dream wedding, and still save money.

Before you commit to any definite plans or budget, take the time to talk with each other and decide together where you could save money or make adjustments. This is the time to talk about the kind of memories you want to create, and the things you value.

If you have a reasonable number of guests, for example, you may be able to hold both the ceremony and the reception in a friend's home or backyard. This would save you a substantial amount of money. Three of our daughters had lovely wedding ceremonies in the elegant backyards of friends and family members. Two of them followed the ceremony with dinner and dancing afterwards ... one on a large patio and pool area, and the other on a dance floor that had been rented for the occasion.

However, don't feel that you will have to limit yourself to home weddings in order to stay within this budget. Other alternatives will be discussed later on, as well.

Once you have come up with some of the areas where you would like to save money, you will be able to redirect that savings towards more lavish expenditures in areas that are important to you. For example, if you save on the reception venue, you could spend a few hundred dollars more for your wedding bands or use the money towards your honeymoon. Play with the numbers, and feel free to change them as you go along. If you find you can save several hundred dollars in one area, feel free to apply it somewhere else, or save it towards your first home, if you prefer!

In every category, the temptation is often to spend every last penny that you have budgeted. Because of this, people frequently end up exceeding their budget when they have unanticipated expenses, such as tips for the service people. It is far better to see how much money you can save in each category. Wouldn't it be nice to budget for a $6,500 wedding and only spend $6,000?

Now that you have personalized the wedding budget to meet your special needs, the next few chapters will contain some ways to find the best prices possible for some of the wedding expenses you will have.

Communicate Inexpensively with Your Guests

As you play around with the amounts you wish to spend on your wedding, you may want to use the Wedding Budgeter that is available at TheKnot.com. You'll find that this website is also a useful place to begin to personalize your wedding plans. Among its attributes, you'll discover that it allows you to post information about your wedding plans on a personalized and private wedding website that you can either set up for free or for only $20 to $30, if you want a personalized web address.

The advantage of setting up your own wedding website is that it will simplify your communications with your friends and relatives as you share information about your wedding plans. The first thing you will want to do is notify your friends and relatives of the existence of your wedding website. If you send out a "save the date" card, you can mention it at the bottom of the card. Another possibility is to send out an email to the people who will be receiving an invitation to the wedding. Tell them about your upcoming nuptials, and let them know they can follow the progress of your plans on your website.

Once you have the website set up, you can use it as a way to tell your story as a couple, post information about where you have registered for wedding gifts, give directions to the wedding venue and pass on other information that you would like to have available to your friends, family and wedding guests. For example, if you have guests who will be coming from out of town, you can add a list of area hotels on your private website for their convenience. If you also include a list of the places where you are registered for gifts, you are more likely to receive some of the household items you would particularly like to receive. By setting up your own free or inexpensive website at The Knot, you will have taken the first steps towards saving money on wedding expenses and, at the same time, you will know that you have passed on all the important information to everyone, without inadvertently overlooking a sensitive relative.

Discount Wedding Dresses

Although there are a large number of bridal boutiques throughout the United States, one company you will want to check out because of their reasonable prices is David's Bridal. Not only do they operate a chain of stores nationwide, but they also have a website with wedding dresses available for as little as $80 - $100. In addition, David's Bridal has an extremely large selection of wedding gowns, both in their stores and online, that retail for $200 to $600. Although it is possible to spend thousands of dollars for a designer wedding gown, it is not necessary to spend that much in order to find a truly elegant, special dress. There are many choices available that are quite affordable.

While you are checking out DavidsBridal.com, you will also want to comparison shop at some of the other websites. Amazon.com has a large selection of wedding gowns from a variety of designers and retailers that are available online for under $500. Other discount online wedding dress stores include WholesaleWeddingGowns.com, and RomanticGowns.com. If you purchase a dress online, be prepared to spend money to have it altered. You will want to allow both the time and some money in your budget for this expense, so you are certain that the dress will fit you perfectly on your wedding day.

If you have your heart set on an expensive designer gown, check out Costco. Yes, that same warehouse store where you can buy television sets and frozen fish, is now hosting a traveling wedding dress trunk show of designer wedding gowns. Even at discount prices, many of the designer dresses from Costco are still priced over $1000. However, if you can't find what you want anywhere else, you may want to find out when the trunk show will be traveling to the Costco store closest to you. Type "wedding dresses" into the search box on Costco.com to find out when the dresses will be available at your local store.

Take your time selecting your wedding dress. This often means that a bride will need to try on a wide variety of dresses to see how she looks in different styles. You will want to do this even if you end up purchasing your dress online. By trying on dresses in person, you will be more qualified to visualize how different styles of dresses will look on you.

Two other places you may wish to visit and try on dresses are consignment shops and thrift stores. Thousands of women resell their wedding dresses at consignment shops every year, and they are often a great place to find an expensive designer dress for a fraction of the original purchase price. Other women simply donate their wedding gowns to thrift stores. I have actually been in a few resale shops that had "boutique" areas where they featured their wedding gowns and evening dresses. If you are very lucky, you may be able to find vintage wedding gowns that were part of an estate. These fabulous antique gowns of silk and lace can be stunning when worn today, especially if you find one that has been lovingly preserved.

If you are looking for a simple white dress, rather than an elaborate gown, you may be able to find one in a department store. Particularly in the spring and summer, it is not unusual to find elegant white suits, sundresses and simple gowns at department store prices, which can sometimes be hundreds of dollars less than similar items sold in fashionable wedding salons.

Another possibility is to purchase a used wedding gown online from eBay or Craig's List. You might have to get it altered, but if you find one at a good enough price, it could be worth it.

If you are patient, do some comparison shopping, and check out both online stores as well as local department stores and consignment shops, you should have ample opportunity to find an elegant wedding dress while staying within your budget.

Discount Bridesmaid Dresses

Bridesmaid dresses are not usually considered part of the wedding expenses that are paid for by the bride or the bride's family. In most cases, the bridesmaids pay for the cost of their gowns themselves. Because of this, it is a wise bride who chooses something the bridesmaids will like, that they might wear again, and that they can afford. Consequently, I wanted to include a chapter about bridesmaids' dresses in this book, as well.

Bridesmaid dresses can be found in many of the same shops as your wedding gown. They are available at David's Bridal Shops,

DavidsBridal.com, Amazon.com and all the other online stores that sell wedding dresses, including WholesaleWeddingGowns.com and RomanticGowns.com. These stores offer a wide range of dresses in a variety of styles, colors and sizes. Bridesmaids' dresses are usually much less expensive than wedding gowns. However, before you make a hasty decision, here are some other suggestions that you might want to consider.

One young woman I knew had several bridesmaids who had all been in weddings before, and they all had at least one pastel colored bridesmaid dress in their closet. The bride simply let the young women wear a pastel colored bridesmaid dress that they already owned! The girls looked lovely as they floated down the aisle in a variety of soft shades of pink, peach and light blue. In addition, they were all pleased and relieved that they did not have to spend more money on another dress that they did not need.

Another bride took her bridesmaids to a popular women's clothing store in the spring, where they picked out a charming sundress that they all liked. This was the dress they wore as bridesmaids. The dresses were all affordable, looked stylish, and were certainly dresses that they could comfortably wear on other occasions.

I have known of other brides who had evening weddings, and asked their bridesmaids to select matching black cocktail dresses to wear to the wedding. The black and white wedding theme was sophisticated, and the bridesmaids were pleased that they had dresses they could happily wear to their next cocktail party or dinner date.

If your bridesmaids can easily afford to buy a traditional bridesmaid dress, then feel comfortable choosing one that pleases you.

However, if your bridesmaids are on a tight budget themselves, or if they really don't want another satin dress that hangs in their closet, you may want to consider being a bit flexible in your choice of bridesmaid dress.

Discount Groom and Groomsmen Clothing

Fortunately, someone figured out decades ago that there is no need for every man to own a tuxedo. A tuxedo is an item that the vast majority of men will only wear rarely, and that will probably be to their own wedding or the weddings of their friends. Even if they do purchase a tuxedo because they expect to wear it again in the future, they might discover that they need a different style of tuxedo, or a different size as the years go by. As a result, one of the most logical ways to obtain a tuxedo for a wedding is to rent one, rather than own one.

One well known company that is ideally set up to help the groom and groomsmen rent their tuxedos is Men's Wearhouse. They have more than 900 locations around the nation. You can pick out the style you want either online or at one of their stores. Then, choose the accessory colors that match the wedding colors. Get the tuxedo fitted at any of their stores. Finally, two days before the ceremony, the guys can pick up their tuxedos at the store that is most convenient to the wedding ceremony. For example, someone could be fitted in Dallas, and pick up their tuxedo in Washington, DC for a Virginia wedding. They advertise tuxedo rentals for as little as $60 per tux. However, in our experience the cost was a bit higher. Despite that, the price was well within the $150 allowed in this budget.

You may also want to comparison shop with local tuxedo rental companies, especially if the groom and groomsmen are all local. Groomsmen will usually rent their own tuxedos.

If the groom and groomsmen already own nice, dark suits, you may want to allow the men to wear those, instead, and save the cost of renting a tuxedo. With a gorgeous silk tie and a boutonniere, you may find that they look just as sophisticated in a dark suit as they would in a tux. This is one of those personal decisions.

Whether or not the guys rent a tux, they may be most comfortable if they wear their own dress shoes. While formal dress shoes can also be rented along with the tux, you will want the men to feel relaxed and comfortable while dancing at your wedding!

Wedding Bands and Engagement Rings

Your wedding band is the one piece of jewelry that you will presumably wear the rest of your life. As a result, this may be an area where you want to splurge a bit. However, there are ways to have a lovely wedding band set, and not break your budget.

Any perusal of Amazon.com will give you a good idea of the selection and price of typical wedding bands that are available for both men and women. For example, women's plain 10k white gold wedding bands can be purchased for under $150. Several designs of titanium bands are available for under $200. Sterling silver wedding bands can be purchased for under $100.

A 14k yellow gold wedding band in styles for either men or women can be purchased for about $250.

You do not have to be satisfied with a plain, smooth wedding band at these prices, either. A titanium wedding ring covered with a band of lab-grade or synthetic diamonds can be purchased for about $150. Bands made from other metals may also be adorned with lab-grade diamonds.

In addition, the metal is often etched with very pretty, intricate designs, such as a Celtic or Victorian pattern. You have many different styles to choose from that are certain to please both the bride and groom.

Take the time to check out other jewelry websites, too. One that I especially like is Zales.com. In addition to their website, you may also want to go into their stores, since they operate a nationwide chain of jewelry stores. They have a nice selection of titanium and stainless steel wedding bands for under $100. You can shop on their site by price, starting with wedding bands under $100, those between $100 and $200, and so on, up to over $1000. Zales also gives you the opportunity to design your own ring. They even offer one style of diamond engagement ring and matching diamond encrusted band for about $300. They also have a large selection of wedding bands and engagement ring sets in the $400 to $700 price range, with up to ½ CT of diamonds set in white or yellow gold.

If you are shopping for a ring set that includes the engagement ring as well as the wedding band, one possibility is to purchase used rings. After all, diamonds have been around for thousands of years, and potentially the stones have had many owners before they were set into your wedding band. You may be able to purchase a used set of wedding bands from a friend, pawn shop or a consignment shop for a fraction of the retail price. It is certainly worth considering, since you may be able to get a good deal on a more valuable ring than you could purchase new in an upscale jewelry store. If you do purchase used rings, you will want to have them appraised so you are certain you know the actual value of the jewelry you are buying. In addition, you may want to have them inspected and repaired if, for example, a stone is loose.

Another possibility is to take a diamond that is already in your family and have it placed in a new setting for your engagement ring. This may not only bring new life to an old piece of family jewelry, but also give sentimental meaning to the bride's new ring, if she uses the stone from a dear relative's antique wedding ring.

Don't forget to be open to precious stones other than diamonds, when you are selecting your engagement ring. Remember that even members of the British royal family have sometimes chosen a sapphire rather than a diamond as the central stone in their engagement ring. If you choose a natural white topaz stone, a genuine amethyst or aquamarine, or a created emerald, as the primary stone, you can save a lot of money and have a beautiful and unique engagement ring. Be creative, and choose a ring set that you will cherish, while staying within your budget.

Save Money on the Wedding and Reception Venues

Where are you going to get married? There are many possibilities. Because nearly half of your budget will be for the church service and reception, this chapter will be one of the most important and the longest in the book.

The best way to save money is to keep your reception simple. However, there is an even more important reason for planning an uncomplicated reception. Not only will most of your money go towards the reception, but most of the stress you experience while planning your wedding will involve the reception. Try to achieve your goal of a wonderful, elegant wedding without going overboard on the reception. Everyone involved in the planning will get along much better! What are some of your choices when planning your wedding and reception venues?

Your first option would be to have the wedding in a church and the reception in another location, such as a restaurant, hotel banquet room, public space, or a private home. Next, you could be married in a church and have a simple reception of appetizers, cake and punch in the fellowship hall of the church immediately following the ceremony. Another choice is to have both the wedding ceremony and the reception in the same location, especially if you are getting married in a private home or a public area, such as a beach or park. There are positive aspects to all of these ideas. Let's examine each of them.

The first choice is to have the wedding at a church, and then invite the guests to another location for the reception. If the reception venue is a private home, you will not be charged for the reception location, although you may incur some costs if you have to rent tables, chairs, dishes and similar items from a party supply company. Depending on your church, and whether or not your family is a member, the price for the church and the minister's fee will probably be quite modest. However, some large cathedrals, such as the National Cathedral in Washington, D.C., can be expensive, and may not even be available for most non-members. In addition, if you are a member of a very large congregation, you might discover there is a long waiting list for an available time and date to use the sanctuary. If you wish to be married in a busy church, you will want to decide on a wedding date and book the church as soon as possible.

If you decide to be married in a church and have the reception somewhere else, consider your options for the reception venue. Three of our daughters were married in the gorgeous backyards of friends or relatives. Two of them had music and dancing after the ceremony. One had a DJ and the dancing took place on the expansive pool deck and patio of the home where the wedding took place. The other daughter had a band and we rented a wooden dance floor that was set up over the lawn to accommodate the dancing. The third daughter decided not to have music and dancing; however, there was an elaborate dinner. All of their weddings were quite lovely and elegant.

However, private homes are not your only choice for an affordable reception venue. There are many other practical reception options as well. For example, you might decide to have your reception in the party room of a hotel or restaurant. Many of them charge very little for the use of the room, if you also hire them to provide the food. Explore the options in your community. In many towns, there are public halls for rent, wedding reception facilities at wineries, and similar choices. Watch your budget carefully, however, if you choose this option. What initially sounds like a good deal may be more expensive than you realize when they start adding on tax, tips, room fees, etc. Make sure you get everything in writing before you make a commitment. In addition, if you use a popular public facility, you may have to reserve the date far in advance.

Don't forget to check out clubhouses where you live. Many condominium associations and gated communities have clubhouses that are available for their residents to use for a low fee. You may have to arrange to have a caterer take care of the food, the set up and the clean up, or have a cleaning service come the next morning, but this could still be a reasonable choice.

The next option you have is to be married in a church and host a simple reception of appetizers, wedding cake and non-alcoholic beverages in the fellowship hall after your wedding ceremony. The same concerns about available dates apply here. If your church hosts frequent weddings, you will want to reserve your date as soon as you possibly can. However, if you decide to have both the wedding and the reception at your church, it is often your most affordable decision. If you have a morning ceremony, you may wish to serve a light lunch. If it is an afternoon wedding, you could follow the ceremony with a light dinner. Since the food will be served buffet style, and little or no liquor can be served in many church reception halls, this is a very inexpensive location for your wedding reception. In many churches you would also be allowed to bring your own appropriate music and have some time for dancing, socializing and enjoying your guests. The cost of using the church and the fellowship hall should be well within your budget, especially if you are a member of the church you are using.

Your third option is to completely opt out of having your ceremony in a church, and celebrate your nuptials at the same location as the wedding reception. For example, you could be married at the beach, in a park, in a backyard, in a large home, or in the chapel or ballroom of a hotel, and have the reception in that location, too. In fact, as long as your minister agrees, you can hold the ceremony anywhere you like.

To explore this option, you may want to start by calling your local parks department. I was married in a city park in Berkeley, California, and I have seen several weddings at public beaches and charming parks in a variety of cities. Often there are popular park pavilions which you may be able to reserve for the day with a very reasonable deposit or fee. You may also be able to find a charming old gazebo in a neighborhood park. There was a park where we lived in Dallas with a lovely and spacious gazebo in the center of it. It was frequently the site of weddings. In Laguna Beach, California, a gazebo that overlooks the ocean is the site of many charming nuptials. If you choose the option of using a park, you may want to hire a caterer to set up the food, and do a little decorating before the ceremony. However, if you have to pay only a small fee to use the park facility, paying a caterer may be well within your budget. You can also ask a few friends and relatives to prepare the space for you, and help remove the decorations afterwards.

I know of several cases where the bride and groom had their "legal" wedding at the county courthouse, and then had a friend read their public vows at a private ceremony with family and friends in the home or other location where the reception was being held. This can be a convenient way to make sure that you have met all the legal requirements, while being able to creatively write your own wedding vows and have the type of ceremony you want. Afterwards, you can celebrate the rest of the day and enjoy the wedding reception with your friends. All the legal requirements were taken care of earlier that day, or even the day before!

When trying to save money on the cost of the wedding and reception venues, there are several things to consider. First, is there a charge for the location or locations that you are using? Will you need to rent supplies, such as extra tables, chairs, dishes, glasses, etc? How much decorating will you need to do? If the venue is already lovely, you may feel that it is not necessary for you to fill the room with floral arrangements. However, if it plain, such as a church reception hall, you may feel the need to spend more money on decorations. Be realistic while you are working on your budget. Make sure you have allowed enough money to cover the cost of the space, as well as party rentals, and decorations.

Next, you need to look at the cost of the food. Are you going to hire caterers who will bring the food, set up the buffet, and provide service people to keep the trays filled, clear the tables, and pour the drinks? Will they clean up everything afterwards? Get an estimate of the cost and ask if it includes the cost of gratuities for the service people. If you are expected to pay a 20% gratuity, this can easily cause you to go over your budget by several hundred dollars. Ask for a written estimate that includes gratuities, taxes and all other expenses.

If the cost of a full-service caterer is too much, see if you can find a restaurant or catering company that will simply drop off the food prior to the wedding reception and leave it in disposable containers that do not have to be returned. This is a workable solution for a buffet style meal as long as you have a few friends or relatives who are willing to transfer the food items to pretty trays and bowls, and make sure they are refilled periodically. The money you can save by eliminating the serving people will be substantial.

Save Money on Alcoholic Beverages

One of the largest expenses at many weddings is the cost of the alcoholic beverages. As a result, I am devoting a separate chapter to dealing with this issue. In the budget at the beginning of this book, we allowed $500 for alcoholic and non-alcoholic beverages for approximately 70 guests. Whether or not this amount of money is adequate will depend on your family, as well as on how many children and other non-drinkers are invited to the reception. This is an issue that you should consider carefully before making your final wedding plans.

First, you can simply decide to have a morning or early afternoon wedding, followed by non-alcoholic beverages only, or just enough champagne for a wedding toast. One of the advantages of this decision is that you will not have to worry about inebriated guests who may try to drive home after getting drunk at your wedding reception. This is your most economical option in dealing with the alcohol issue. However, I realize that many people want their wedding reception to be an exciting party and, for them, alcoholic beverages are an important part of the festivities.

Another way to stay within your budget for alcohol is to place bottles of red and white wine on each table, and have either bottled beer or a beer keg with mugs available on a side table. When it is time for the formal wedding toasts, have someone set out pre-filled glasses of champagne, so no guests help themselves to an entire bottle. With this arrangement, you will know specifically how much you are spending on the alcohol, and you can make your beer, wine and champagne choices based on staying within your budget. You can plan to have an adequate amount of alcohol for everyone to enjoy the evening, without providing an excessive amount. Of course, some people will always drink more than others, but they will still be limited by the amount that was originally purchased.

A more expensive option is to hire a bartender and provide him with enough alcohol and mixers to allow him to create a variety of cocktails. He would also pour the beer, wine and champagne, which means that guests would go up to him to refill their glasses one at a time, instead of serving themselves. If you provide no more alcohol than you want served, you can control your costs. Don't forget that, with this choice, you will have the additional expense of the bartender and his gratuity. The cost of the bartender will take up a large part of the amount that you have budgeted for alcohol.

However you decide to handle the question of alcoholic beverages, you want to be certain you have a large supply of non-alcoholic beverages available, too. In most families, at least some of your guests will be non-drinkers.

If you are trying to control the cost of your reception, the worst thing you can do is to have an open bar with an unlimited supply of alcohol. This frequently occurs when weddings are held at restaurants and hotels. Some guests who are heavy drinkers can run up a surprisingly large bill for alcoholic beverages by ordering more and more drinks from the waiters at the restaurant or hotel. Before you know it, 50 or more guests can easily run up a bar bill of $1000 or more.

Anytime you are trying to stay within a budget, you want to be sure you have a system for controlling your expenses so you are absolutely certain that you cannot exceed the budgeted amount. It is quite easy to let wedding expenses run away from you, especially where alcohol is involved.

Save Money on Flowers

Flowers are an integral part of most weddings, and nearly every bride will want a lovely bouquet for herself, small nosegays for her attendants, boutonnieres for the groom and groomsmen, and a few other flower arrangements for the reception. You may also wish to purchase corsages for the mothers of the bride and groom, and boutonnieres for their fathers. There are several ways you can save money on flowers.

First, is there a wholesale flower market in your area? Many large cities have one and, with a little advance research, you may discover a wholesale florist who can provide all the bouquets and floral arrangements for your wedding at a reasonable price. They might not deliver, so someone will need to pick up the flowers that morning. However, the savings could be substantial.

If this doesn't work, you may need to decide which flowers are the most important to you. For example, you may discover that the arrangement that is most important to you is the bridal bouquet. If this is true for you, concentrate on spending most of your money on that item. I have been to several weddings where the bridesmaids carried only a simple white or pink long-stemmed rose. The bridesmaids looked lovely, and the flowers were far less expensive than a complicated nosegay for each bridesmaid.

As for the floral arrangements that are used for centerpieces, keep them simple and small. Many brides choose elaborate centerpieces that end up being set on the floor because they make it difficult for the guests at the tables to see around them. Most guests will greatly appreciate it if their table is decorated with a small, brightly colored arrangement that they can easily see over. The arrangements do not need to be expensive, either. For example, you could buy a selection of small vases at a local Dollar Store and fill them the morning of the wedding with lots of greenery and a few elegant roses or other in-season flowers. This will brighten up the room, and not be too elaborate or too expensive. You can also talk to the florist who is creating the bridal bouquet and ask her what types of simple floral arrangements she could provide for about $20 each. I have known of some florists who will refund a deposit fee if you return the vases or decorative containers after the wedding.

Another alternative for the cost-conscious bride is to use faux flower bouquets and arrangements. This is very common at some of the wedding chapels in Las Vegas, as well as in other areas. Often wedding chapels will loan the bride a faux flower arrangement to carry down the aisle. Even if the bride decides she wants to carry a real floral bouquet, her bridesmaids could carry silk flowers, instead. If you have a young flower girl, a little basket full of artificial flowers may be the most practical idea, as she might be careless with real flowers, anyway.

You may also decide to use silk flowers for your centerpieces rather than real flowers. In this way, the centerpieces could be created weeks in advance and simply placed on the tables the morning of the wedding. Some hotels, restaurants and caterers can also provide faux floral arrangements that could be used as table centerpieces. This is an inexpensive, simple and attractive way to have abundant flower arrangements at your wedding reception.

If your wedding is being held in a private home, it is possible that the outdoor landscaping and the floral arrangements already inside the home will more than meet your floral needs. In this way, the bride can have a bouquet, and very few additional flowers will even be necessary. Many restaurants and other settings may also be so well decorated, that additional decorations are unnecessary.

Discounts on Groomsmen Gifts

One or more of the groom's friends will serve as the Best Man and the groomsmen. They will probably arrange a bachelor party for him, and may incur the personal expense of renting tuxedos or traveling to the ceremony. As a result, it is thoughtful to provide them with a little gift or memento of your wedding day. However, if you are trying to save money on your wedding, you do not want to go overboard. How can you buy them something thoughtful, and still save money?

First, think about the ways the groom and groomsmen have enjoyed spending time together in the past. Do they all support a favorite sports team? Purchasing them ball caps or jerseys in their team colors, or with the team logo, can be a fun gift the guys will really enjoy.

There are also online shops that specialize in providing great groomsmen gifts at reasonable prices. Some of the sites you may want to check out are DavidsBridal.com, Beau-coup.com, Wrapwithus.com and TheKnot.com. Of course, if you know specifically what you want to buy the guys, any shop will work, including your local sporting goods store.

Among the types of groomsmen gifts that are advertised on the above mentioned websites are: dolphin bottle openers (for a beach wedding), crystal sailboats, personalized beer koozies, horseshoe key chains, groomsman champagne flutes and stainless steel martini shakers. These websites have a large selection of available items for under $20, and an even larger selection for just a few dollars more.

No matter what you decide to purchase, keep it fun and reasonably priced. The most important gift you can give them is to let them know how much you appreciate their help and support on your wedding day. Consequently, don't forget to tell them that! The bride and groom should write the groomsmen a personal thank you note, telling them how much you appreciate everything they have done to make your day special. Your note will mean as much as any gift you could give them.

Discounts on Bridesmaid Gifts

Another group of friends who deserve a little gift of appreciation are the bridesmaids. They may have thrown you a wedding shower or a bachelorette party. They have probably shopped with you, giggled with you and given you lots of supportive hugs. Almost certainly they have spent money to purchase bridesmaid dresses, shoes and other items necessary in order to be part of your wedding. They also deserve a little token of your appreciation, as well as a note of your sincere thanks.

When you are shopping for your wedding gown, keep an eye open for possible bridesmaid gifts. Many shops like David's Bridal have an area devoted to attendant gifts. You can also find gifts online, or at department stores like Macy's and Nordstrom's.

There are many different approaches to bridesmaid gifts. Perhaps the most common gift for the bridesmaids is an item of jewelry that they all wear to the wedding. For example, you might want to purchase each of them a strand of faux pearls, or a simple heart-shaped pendant necklace. You may also want them to have matching earrings to go with their necklaces. Jewelry is something that you know your bridesmaids will wear again and, when they do, they will think of you.

One store that frequently has jewelry on sale is Macy's. Nearly every month, but particularly just before Valentine's Day and Christmas, they have sales on their boxed jewelry sets. Among the items they frequently have on sale are heart shaped pendants with matching earrings, often at extremely reasonable prices. Watch for sales in your area, and see if you can find the perfect jewelry set to go with the dresses the bridesmaids will be wearing. You will also want to check out other department stores in your area, too.

Jewelry is not the only gift you may want your bridesmaids to have. The website Beau-coup.com also offers a selection of charming bridesmaid items such as personalized canvas weekender tote bags, bracelets, scarves and shawls. You might also purchase pretty wedding ballet-style slip-on shoes for the bridesmaids, so they can slip out of their heels while they are dancing at the reception.

One popular item is the bridesmaid survival kit. You can purchase these already pre-made, or put together your own. Some of the items you may want to include are a mirror, hair brush, hair spray, hairpins, stain remover, earring backs, and anything else that might be lost or forgotten on your wedding day. With this thoughtful gift, none of the bridesmaids will be in a panic when they misplace their hair brush or lose an earring back. If you aren't sure what to put in the survival kit, purchase a ready made one from DavidsBridal.com.   Whatever you decide, it is a thoughtful and practical gift.

Another possibility for the bridesmaids is to shop at a Things Remembered kiosk in your local mall, or at ThingsRemembered.com. They have a wide selection of items that can be personalized. You can order each of your bridesmaids a personalized champagne flute, or an engraved picture frame. They also have items of jewelry and other gifts that are perfect for the bridesmaids.

Whatever gift you choose, give it along with a hug and a note telling them how important they were in helping to make your day special. Knowing that you appreciate them will mean much more than your gifts alone.

One additional thought for the bride and groom: you will also want to write a note and give a gift of appreciation to your parents. Let them know how much you appreciate everything they have done for you both. Gifts can be purchased at many of the same places where you purchased your attendant gifts. Your parents will really appreciate your thoughtfulness.

Discount Wedding Favors

I cannot emphasize enough that there is absolutely no reason why you should feel it is necessary to give your guests a wedding favor. I have been to dozens of weddings during my lifetime, and cannot remember a single wedding favor that I received. I am sure this is true for most people. However, if you feel it is absolutely necessary to give your guests a little token on your wedding day, you will want to spend as little as possible, and keep it simple.

Begin your search for wedding favors by shopping online, unless you know of a great discount shop or wholesaler in your area. Some of the online businesses you may want to try are favorsbyserendipity.com and Wrapwithus.com. Both sites have some clever wedding favors that can be purchased for only $2 - $3 per item.

Examples of party favors that are appealing are silver sailboat place card holders, small monogrammed gift bags that you can fill with candy, tiny picture frame place card holders, picture frame coasters, and little boxes. You can even purchase little monogrammed jars of jam, monogrammed boxes of candy, miniature cakes and candles. Scroll through the online gift sites and see the hundreds of possible wedding favors they have available, and choose one that goes with your wedding theme.

Remember, a wedding favor is not necessary, and should only be purchased if you have room in your budget. If you find yourself running over your budget in other areas, wedding favors are one expense you can eliminate entirely.

Instead, you could simply set place cards at each

table, if you decide to have assigned seats.

Wedding Reception Songs

Many brides dream about dancing with the man of their dreams on their wedding day. Although having a wedding DJ arrange the music for your reception may be a nice luxury, thanks to modern technology it is not really a necessary expense, despite the fact that we have allowed $300 in the budget, just in case you do decide to use one.

Instead of a DJ, however, you can save money at your wedding reception by putting together your own play list and hooking your iPod or other MP3 player up to stereo speakers or a sound system. If you have a friend who is willing to monitor the iPod from time to time during the evening, you may be able to have great music without needing to hire a DJ. All the friend would need to do is turn it off when people want to make toasts or announcements, and restart it when everyone wants to dance. This is especially convenient if you are having your reception in an intimate setting such as a home or restaurant, where you won't want the music blasting at top volume, anyway.

If you decide to put together your own play list, you may be uncertain what songs you should include. This uncertainty is one reason people use wedding DJ's in the first place. However, you do not need to feel intimidated. You can choose your wedding reception music weeks in advance and test everything out, so you are certain you have chosen enough music, and it works well with the sound system you are using.

First, of course, you will want to select a romantic song that will be appropriate for your First Dance together. Then, you will want to include songs for the Father-Daughter and Mother-Son dances. All of these songs are usually slow dances.

Once you have gotten the formalities out of the way, you will want to select additional songs that will be popular with a variety of generations. This means that you will want to combine the music that your generation enjoys with songs that will delight your parents and grandparents, as well.

To get you started, here are some popular songs for different parts of your reception:

First Dance Songs for the Bride and Groom

Can You Feel the Love Tonight (Elton John)

Close to You (The Carpenters)

Embraceable You (Nat King Cole)

Forever (Kenny Loggins)

At Last (Etta James)

Because You Loved Me (Celine Dion)

Unforgettable (Nat King Cole)

You Are So Beautiful (Joe Croker)

May I Have This Dance for the Rest of My
Life (Anne Murray)

Father-Daughter Dance Songs

My Girl (The Temptations)

Butterfly Kisses (Bob Carlisle)

I Loved Her First (Heartland)

What a Wonderful World (Louis Armstrong)

My Wish (Rascal Flatts)

Mother–Son Dance Songs

The Man You've Become (Celine Dion)

A Song for Mama (Boys II Men)

Angels (Randy Travis)

A Song for My Son (Rita Heatherington)

My Wish (Rascal Flatts)

Popular Dance Songs for All Ages

All Night Long (Lionel Richie)

Twist and Shout (The Isley Brothers)

Kokomo (The Beach Boys)

Blinded by Love (The Rolling Stones)

One Love (Bob Marley)

The Way You Look Tonight (Frank Sinatra)

Wonderful Tonight (Eric Clapton)

I Will Always Love You (Whitney Houston)

Take Me Home, Country Roads (John
Denver)

Ain't No Other Man (Christina Aguilera)

At Last (Etta James)

Can't Help Falling in Love With You (Corey
Hart)

In addition to these songs, you and your
fiancé may already have a favorite dance song. In
that case, you will certainly want to use it. You
might also ask your parents if they have
suggestions for the Father-Daughter or Mother-
Son dances. My husband spent hours choosing
songs for his last Father-Daughter dance.

If you can't think of anything on your own,
the above list will be a great place to start. Of
course, some of these songs will seem quite old-
fashioned to a young couple. However, if you mix
a few of these tunes in with the music that you

and your friends love, the older guests at your reception will really appreciate listening to a few of their old favorites. One other thoughtful gesture would be to ask your parents and grandparents if they have one song that they would really like to hear at your wedding.

By the time you have put together your play list, you may be surprised to discover you have more than enough music to fill the evening!

Cheap Wedding Invitations

One way you can save money is to be cautious about how much money you spend on your wedding invitations and thank you notes. Since postage is approaching $.50 a letter, you will probably want your invitations to cost less than a total of $140, and your thank you notes should cost no more than about $35, if you want to stay within the budget we set up earlier of $200 total for invitations and $60 total for thank you notes. This allows you to spend $30 postage to mail out 60 invitations, $30 postage for the RSVP cards, and $25 postage to mail out 50 thank you notes, which should be adequate. In fact, if you are expecting about 70 people to come to your wedding, you will probably send out approximately 40 - 50 invitations, since many people will come as couples, some will not be able to attend, and others will come alone, without a date.

Start the invitation process with an enthusiastic e-mail announcing your wedding plans months in advance. In this way, you can probably avoid having to send out Save the Date cards, which would add another $40 or $50 to your total expenses, when you include the necessary $25 for postage. In your e-mail you should include a link to your wedding webpage at TheKnot.com. Your webpage will provide much more information than any Save The Date card possibly could, since you will be able to use it to give wedding and reception details, hotel information, and the list the stores where you are registered.

Although sending an e-mail to friends and family to announce your upcoming wedding plans would be appropriate, you should not send an email as a replacement for the actual wedding invitation. In fact, you should mention in your email that that the email recipients will all be receiving invitations a few weeks prior to the wedding. That way, there is no doubt in their mind that they are invited. Then, you need to select and order your invitations and RSVP cards. It will take a few weeks to receive them, address them, and prepare them to be mailed out. Once you have the invitations in the mail, you can send out another email letting people know about any updates to your wedding website; you can also mention that the invitations are on the way! Since many people are absolutely horrible about sending in their RSVP's, you may want to give them the option of responding by email.

When shopping for your invitations, there are many online companies that can prepare personalized wedding invitations at discount prices. A company called annsbridalbargains.com offers attractive invitations for about $40 to $90 for a box of 100. This is well within the budgeted amount of $140, but you are probably purchasing more invitations than you will need.

If there is a Hallmark Card shop in your area, they could also assist you with your wedding invitations, at a reasonable price. Hallmark.com have invitations available online. Most of the invitations cost about $1.80 each, but you can get a discount if you buy a large enough quantity of them. You will want to evaluate if you are better off purchasing only the number of invitations you need, and paying more per card, or if it is more economical to save money by purchasing a larger quantity of cards. Hallmark also offers some special services that could be helpful if you are overwhelmed with all your wedding plans. For an additional charge, Hallmark can arrange to address, stamp and mail your cards for you. You just send them the list of names and addresses.

Another possibility is to buy your own wedding invitation stationery at the office supply store, and print the invitations up on your home computer. A company called Icipaper.com actually sells a wide selection of printable wedding invitation cards at reasonable prices. Office Max also sells a selection of printable wedding invitations, and so do many other paper and office supply companies. This can be an economical way to save money on your invitations. However, do not attempt to print your own invitations unless you are comfortable with your ability to produce professional looking invitations. If you are

unhappy with the finished product, and end up

throwing them out and ordering the invitations

from someone else, you will not have saved

anything. You are the best judge of your

capabilities.

Save Money on Wedding Photos

It is not unusual for some couples to spend between $1000 and $2000 for wedding photos, so having a $350 budget for this item may seem unreasonably small. How in the world can you keep the expense so low?

First, concentrate on getting formal shots of just the poses that are most important to you. In particular, you will want a photo of the bride by herself, the bride and groom together, the bride and groom with their wedding party, the bride with her attendants, the bride with her family, the groom with his attendants, and the groom with his family. You may want to have more than one pose for each of these photos, especially the bride and groom together, so you have several different ones to frame, put on your first Christmas card, etc.

Contact wedding photographers in your area and tell them your budget for their services, including prints of the finished photos. Let them know you also want the rights to the photos, so you can use them for your holiday cards or to make additional copies. Find a photographer who is willing to come to the wedding ceremony for an hour to take those formal shots, and then provide you with the prints. If necessary, you may even arrange for the bride, groom and their families to go to the photographer's studio to be photographed there, if it is going to be too expensive to have the photographer come to the wedding.

Many photographers will now download the finished photos to a disk that can be used to access the photos on your home computer. Other photographers have a website where you can access and download the photos you want. In most cases, you will need to carefully limit your time with the professional photographer. He will charge much more if you also want him to spend the evening at the reception, so try to get the minimum package he will provide.

Of course, in addition to the professional photos, you will still want to have candid photos of the reception. Ask your guests to provide those photographs. Many guests will be happy to use their own cameras or camera phones to photograph their favorite moments during the ceremony and reception. Ask at least one person to be sure to get photos of the two of you cutting the cake, dancing your First Dance together, and enjoying the wedding toasts. Family members are likely to be especially responsible about insuring that the most important photos are taken. The bride and groom may want to take a few pictures of their family and friends, as well.

After the ceremony, ask your guests to email you their favorite photos. Once you have a nice selection, use an online site like Snapfish to create your own, glossy professional looking wedding album. Between the album you create, and the professional photos provided by the photographer, you will have a nice collection of wedding photos without spending an excessive amount of money.

You also will need to decide if you want a professional video of the ceremony, or if you can simply ask a friend to videotape it. There is money in the budget, although this may be another area you decide is unnecessary. Many wedding videos have been ruined by a crying child during the ceremony or a drunken guest during the reception.

Save Money on Wedding Gift Bags

Do you have out of town guests who will be traveling to your wedding? If so, it is considered a thoughtful gesture for the bride and groom to provide them with a gift bag of "goodies" to show how much you appreciate the effort your guests went to in order to attend your wedding. Here is how to put together gift bags that will be appreciated and won't cost you a large amount of money.

Start with either a colorful paper gift bag from the Dollar Store or a small canvas tote bag, if you can find an inexpensive one.

Inside the bag, you will want to include at least some of the items listed below. Many of these items will cost you little or nothing, so be generous with those things that you can include for free. Presenting your out-of-town guests with a gift bag will go a long way towards making your guests feel appreciated, especially if you do not have much time to visit with them personally during your busy wedding weekend.

Here are some things you may want to include:

An agenda for the weekend's activities, so they know where they are supposed to go, the times, and the directions;

A personal note thanking your guests for coming;

Information they might find helpful during their stay (brochures from local restaurants, flyers about special events going on in town, information about tourist attractions, museums, etc.)

Local food items, such as candy, honey, cookies, jams, etc.

Local souvenir items such a small paperback cookbook, postcards, key chains, coffee mugs, etc.

A bottle of water;

A small emergency kit, with items like spot remover, Pepto-Bismol, toothpaste, band-aids, Advil, safety pins, sun screen and anything else you think they might need.

Your out-of-town guests will appreciate your thoughtfulness and your gift bag will make them feel welcome and appreciated.

Final Thoughts

Remember that this is your wedding and, hopefully, the only one you will ever have. As a result, you want it to be the type of wedding that you always envisioned, as long as you stay within your budget. Be inventive in finding ways to create the look you want as economically as possible.

I have known brides who have borrowed flowering potted plants from friends, to create a more lavish floral display than they could otherwise afford. I have also known brides who got together with their friends the day before the wedding to wind strings of white lights around tree branches and porch rails to create a soft light for their evening outdoor wedding.

In other cases, brides and their relatives have spent weeks creating unique centerpieces to use on their tables, requiring that only a little fresh greenery be added the day before their nuptials.

Some families have talented friends who are willing to sing at the wedding, play an instrument during the ceremony, or put together a fabulous wedding album using their own photographs.

One of our daughters had a bridesmaid who was also a gifted jewelry designer. She made each of the other bridesmaids a unique necklace to wear. The jewelry was her wedding gift to our daughter; it also served as gifts to the bridesmaids.

The bottom line is that some of your family and friends will be delighted to assist you in making your wedding day special, if you let them. When you do, you will enrich not only your own day, but you will make them feel special, as well.

Be sure to let them know how much you

appreciate everyone's help.

May all your wedding dreams come true!

15 Helpful Websites

While making your wedding plans, you may want to check out some of the websites mentioned in this book. This author has no connection to any of these websites. They are simply sites that members of my own family have used, or they are sites that have a nice selection of wedding items at reasonable prices. Since these sites were mentioned separately in different spots throughout this book, here is a list of all of them in one place:

DavidsBridal.com

TheKnot.com

WholesaleWeddingGowns.com

RomanticGowns.com

Costco.com

Amazon.com

Zales.com

Beau-coup.com

Wrapwithus.com

ThingsRemembered.com

Favorsbyserendipity.com

Annsbridalbargains.com

Hallmark.com

Icipaper.com

Snapfish.com